The Ancient World For Kids

A History Series

Children Explore History Book Edition

SPEEDY
PUBLISHING

Speedy Publishing LLC
40 E. Main St. #1156
Newark, DE 19711
www.speedypublishing.com

Every country have its own rich history, read and learn some of the country's discoverers!

Australia

Discovered on 1688
Discovered by
Captain James Cook

Brazil

Discovered on 1500
Discovered by
Pedro Álvares Cabral

Canada

Discovered on 1534
Discovered by
Jacques Cartier

Chile

Discovered on 1520
Discovered by
Diego de Almagro

Colombia

Discovered on 1492
Discovered by
Christopher Columbus

Cuba

Discovered on 1492
Discovered by
Christopher Columbus

Ecuador

Discovered on 1531
Discovered by
Francisco Pizarro

Guatemala

Discovered on 1524
Discovered by Pedro
de Alvarado

Honduras

Discovered on 1502
Discovered by
Christopher Columbus

Iceland

Discovered on 9th century
Discovered by
Naddoddr

India

Discovered on 1498
Discovered by
Vasco da Gama

Jamaica

Discovered on 1494
Discovered by
Christopher Columbus

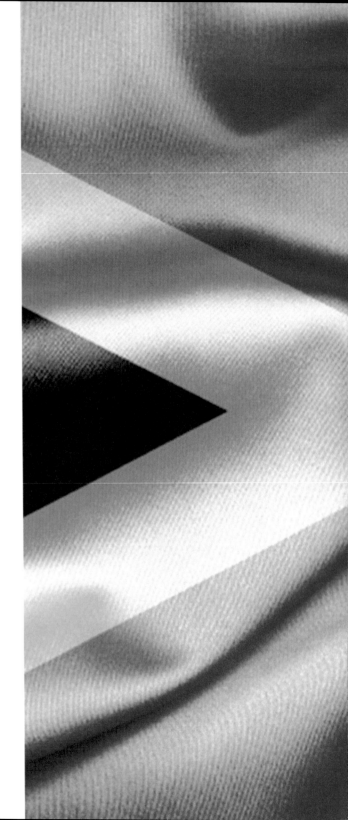

Mexico

Discovered on 1518
Discovered by
Hernan Cortes

Peru

Discovered on 1513
Discovered by
Francisco Pizarro

Philippines

Discovered on 1521
Discovered by
Ferdinand Magellan

Russia

Discovered on 862
Discovered by
Viking Rurik

Singapore

Discovered on 1819
Discovered by
Thomas Stamford Raffles

Venezuela

Discovered on 1498
Discovered by
Christopher Columbus

Made in the USA
Lexington, KY
22 August 2018